more posers

drawings by jo ann stover

80 intriguing new hurdles
for reasonably
agile minds

MORE POSERS

by

philip kaplan

harper & row, publishers

new york, evanston, and london

to Joan and Robert

introduction

The purpose of this introduction is to state briefly what you will find in the body of the book and, more basically, to explain what a poser is. First, however, let me explain what a poser isn't. It isn't a trick, a riddle or a puzzle and it isn't a problem which is solved by knowing certain scientific, mathematical or other facts. For example, you don't have to know that a man wearing glasses on a cold night who walks into a hot, damp room will temporarily be sightless because of fog on his lenses; that a vital document (or even a useless one) can't be hidden between pages 17 and 18 of a book because they aren't facing pages; you don't even have to know that Cypripedium is a genus of the Orchid family.

What is a poser? It is a statement of facts from which a person, without special knowledge, can reason to a logical conclusion. *More Posers,* in purpose and arrangement, is similar to its predecessor, *Posers* (published in 1963). Again, only common sense, properly exercised and directed, is necessary to solve the posers which are arranged in eight groups of ten and, within each group, in approximate order of difficulty. If you want a numerical determination of your poser-solving ability, score cards are printed at the end of each group for this purpose. Score 10 points if you get the right answer within the time limit allowed, 7 points if you take up to twice the prescribed time and 3 points if you take more time than that.

Better yet, don't worry about your score, just enjoy the excitement and satisfaction of resolving eighty intriguing challenges to your intellect and imagination. Then, if you are not asocial, the book can be put to very good use as a party starter *par excellence.* Your only problem will be to wean your guests away from posers onto some other fascinating subject such as a discussion about your children or local gossip.

As already mentioned, special training and particularly mathematical knowledge, other than the simplest arithmetic, are not needed to cope with these posers. However, the logical mind which gets directly to the root of things—a quality of mind claimed for themselves by most people—is just what is needed.

Speaking of logical analysis and common sense, a friend of mine who enjoys a drink or two before dinner, was advised by his physician to give up intoxicants as a health measure. Being also fond of logic, he decided to analyze the facts before taking such a drastic step. His analysis showed that the distressing symptoms which prompted the consultation with his doctor occurred whenever he drank rye and water, Scotch and water, or bourbon and water. Naturally, he decided to give up water, which common sense indicated was the cause of his trouble. The fact that his symptoms have grown worse will, I am sure, have some deep significance for the philosophical reader.

The next to last (seventh) group of posers is different from the others. In this set, "game" or "position" situations have been described and diagrammed and you are asked to get to the root of the situation to determine the winning move or to arrive at a certain end position.

The final group is also special, containing a selection of very interesting but particularly difficult posers (super posers). Don't be surprised if you have to look up most of the answers to these in the back of the book where, incidentally, detailed answers to all the posers will be found.

poser group one

score 10, 7, 3 or 0
score card on page 8

1.

If it costs $100 to paint the 2 lines which divide a certain street into 3 broad traffic lanes, how much would it cost to paint the lines necessary to create 6 traffic lanes on a similar street?

2 minutes

2.

Six glasses are standing in a row. The first 3 are empty while the last 3 are full of water. By handling and moving only 1 glass, it is possible to change this arrangement so that no empty glass is next to another empty one and no full glass is next to another full glass.

How is this done?

5 minutes

3.

At the end of a one-way street is a river. To prevent
cars from going over the embankment, a fence has been
erected and on it is a sign reading DEAD END. Cars are
parked on both sides of the street, all facing east toward
the river. A man who lives on the street notices that all
the parking spaces on both sides of the street are occupied.

There is a basic impossibility in the above, fancied
description. What is it?

4 minutes

4.

Using 6 cigarettes of equal length, how can they be arranged so that 4 triangles are formed whose sides are the length of the cigarettes?

HINT: *The cigarettes do not all have to lie on one surface.*

5 minutes

5.

A gambler makes an "even money" bet on the toss of a coin. The amount he bets is half the amount of money he has in his possession. Win or lose, he then again bets half the amount of money he has at that time. This process continues until 10 bets have been made, 5 of which the gambler wins.

Is the gambler ahead, even or behind after the 10th bet?

7 minutes

6.

Window cleaners sometimes work in teams, one man washing insides only while the other does the outsides. On a particular day, one man came to work early and had already washed 4 insides when his partner arrived and reminded him that he was supposed to be the "outside" man that day. The latecomer then took over the work on the insides while the early bird started on the outsides. When the inside man completed all the remaining insides, he helped the outside man finish by washing 8 outsides.

If we consider an inside or an outside to be 1 window, who washed more windows that day, and how many more did he wash?

7 minutes

7.

Between 2 pieces of paper, a conventional piece of carbon paper is placed with the carbon side facing down in the usual manner. The papers are then folded in half so that the lower part rests beneath the upper half. Now someone writes on the exposed surface of the original paper and, of course, the writing will appear on the upper half of the duplicate copy as well.

Will the writing on the lower half be on the original or duplicate, on the front or back, and will the writing be as written or otherwise? (No papers or carbon allowed.)

10 minutes

8.

On a shoe rack there are a total of 12 shoes consisting of 3 identical pairs of black and 3 identical pairs of brown shoes. They have been put on the rack in a completely mixed up pattern.

If the color of the shoes cannot be seen because of insufficient light but one can tell a "left" from a "right" by feel, how many shoes must be selected to assure that among the selection will be a pair of black or brown shoes?

10 minutes

9.

Two children intended to share the contents of a large glass which was filled to the top with juice. One child had drunk a portion of the contents when the question arose whether or not the remainder was more, less, or just half the contents of the glass.

Assuming that the children had no measuring devices, in fact had no equipment whatsoever, how could they easily determine whether the first child had had his proper share, too much, or too little?

10 minutes

10.

King Solomon is reputed to have solved a poser involving the equitable division of a piece of land by having one man divide it into two halves and the other select the half he wanted.

If a piece of land is to be divided equitably among three men, how can this division be made so that each man will be satisfied that he has at least ⅓ of the total? (There is more than one solution to this poser but the one desired is that which is applicable to a division among any number of men.)

45 minutes

poser group one score

1 _____		6 ———	
2 _____		7 _____	
3 _____		8 _____	
4 _____		9 _____	
5 _____		10 _____	

total score _____

Poser I. Q.
About 50 is average
65-75 is exceptional
Over 75 is outstanding

poser group two

score 10, 7, 3 or 0
score card on page 16

11.

Two boys are rowing around in a stream, in a small boat, when six men approach one bank and ask if they can use the boat to get to the opposite bank. It is soon determined, however, that although the boat can hold two boys, it can hold no more than one man.

How can the six men get to the other side under these conditions?

3 minutes

12.

Two clocks show the correct time to be twelve o'clock. One clock is running properly; the other is also running at the correct rate, but backwards.

When is the next time that both clocks will show the same time?

3 minutes

13.

Two candles of equal length are lit at the same time. One candle takes 6 hours and the other 3 hours to burn out.

After how much time will the slower burning candle be exactly twice as long as the faster burning one?

4 minutes

14.

Three cards from an ordinary deck are lying on a table, face down. The following information (for some peculiar reason) is known about the cards:

1. To the left of a Queen, there is a Jack.
2. To the left of a Spade, there is a Diamond.
3. To the right of a Heart, there is a King.
4. To the right of a King, there is a Spade.

Can you assign the proper suit to each picture card?

7 minutes

15.

By using which of the following means will a bathtub full of water be emptied faster:

1. One circular outlet, 2″ in diameter, or
2. Two circular outlets, each 1″ in diameter?

4 minutes

16.

In response to a question about whose portrait was hanging on the wall, a man replies in this roundabout way. "The father of the person in the portrait is my father's son, but I have no brothers or sons."

If the responder had given a direct answer, what would he have said?

7 minutes

17.

You are driving along a 3-lane, one-way highway with traffic moving slowly, when you see a sign reading, 2-LANE TRAFFIC AHEAD. The sign does not indicate, nor can you see whether the left or right lane is going to disappear. Since you are in a hurry, you would like to avoid as much delay as possible.

Which lane, left, middle, or right, should you travel in and why?

4 minutes

18.

A man wants to ship a rifle which is about a yard and a half in length by motor express. He finds, however, that the regulations covering express shipments do not allow any dimension of a package to be more than one yard in length.

Without altering the rifle in any way, what can the man do so that he can ship it without violating the shipping regulations?

5 minutes

19.

Two ships which had left New York and Liverpool at the same time, pass each other at sea. The ship from New York reaches Liverpool 1 day after the meeting, while the Liverpool ship reaches New York 4 days after the meeting.

If both ships are traveling at uniform rates, how much faster is one ship going than the other?

15 minutes

20.

Assume that a man can carry a maximum of 4 days' supply of food and water for a journey over a desert which takes 6 days to cross. Obviously, one man cannot make the trip alone because he would run out of food and water after 4 days.

How many men would have to start out in order for one man to get across and for the other (or others) to get back to the starting point?

15 minutes

poser group two score

11 _____		16 _____
12 _____		17 _____
13 _____		18 _____
14 _____		19 _____
15 _____		20 _____

total score _____

Poser I. Q.
About 50 is average
*   65-75 is exceptional*
Over 75 is outstanding

poser group three

score 10, 7, 3 or 0
score card on page 24

21.

A drawer contains 10 identical brown socks and 10 identical black socks.

How many socks must one take from the drawer (assuming it's too dark to see the color) to be sure of having a pair of brown socks?

2 minutes

22.

A certain city is divided into 10 taxi zones numbered consecutively from 1 to 10. Taxi fare within a zone is 50¢, but if a trip extends into another zone the fare is 50¢ for each zone plus an extra charge of 40¢ for crossing a zone boundary. Thus, a trip involving 3 zones normally costs $1.50 (3 zones) plus 80¢ (2 boundaries) or $2.30.

One day a man wanted to go from the middle of zone 1, through zone 2, and to the middle of zone 3, a trip which, as indicated above, should cost $2.30. When he found that he didn't have that much money with him, he improvised a way to make the taxi trip (at a slight inconvenience to himself) for less.

What did he do?

5 minutes

23.

A merchant sold a bookcase for $40.00 and then repurchased it for $30.00. He then sold it again for $35.00. How much money did he make—$5.00, $10.00, $15.00, or can the amount of his profit or loss not be determined?

8 minutes

24.

A ship can travel 30 miles an hour in still water. With a favoring wind the ship can go 45 miles an hour, but traveling into the wind its speed is reduced to 15 miles an hour.

As compared with a round trip of 30 miles each way in still water, would it take more time, less time, or the same time to make the same round trip first against the wind and then with the wind?

5 minutes

25.

Two automobiles start out together on a ten-mile trip. Both cars travel at uniform speeds, but one travels twice as fast as the other.

Is there a time during the trip when the slower car has 5,000 times as far to go as the faster car?

10 minutes

26.

The police were convinced that either A, B, C or D had committed a crime. Each of the suspects, in turn, made a statement, but only one of the four statements was true.

A said, "I didn't do it."

B said, "A is lying."

C said, "B is lying."

D said, "B did it."

Who committed the crime?

12 minutes

27.

A man went into a store to make an $8.00 purchase but found that he was a little short of cash. Instead of borrowing the exact amount he needed to buy the item, he borrowed an amount equal to the amount he already had. After making the purchase, he went to another store where he repeated the process, again borrowing the amount he already had and buying something for $8.00. After repeating this procedure a third time, the man had no money left.

How much money did he start with?

10 minutes

28.

A man sitting on a tree stump at the side of a deep lake has been pulling his son across the lake by means of a very long rope attached to a raft on which the son is sitting. As the raft reaches the center of the lake, the knot holding the rope to the raft gets untied, the rope sinks to the bottom, and the raft is marooned in the middle of the lake.

The raft is too far out for the man to throw the rope to the boy; neither the boy nor the father can swim; the raft cannot be propelled by the boy in any way; and the father has no equipment whatsoever other than that already mentioned.

How does the father bring his son safely to shore under these adverse conditions?

5 minutes

29.

How can five identical coins be placed so that every coin touches every other coin?

20 minutes

30.

In a certain community, the inhabitants were of two classes, those who always told the truth (Class A) and those who always lied (Class B). A stranger found himself in this community at a point in the road where it forked, one fork leading to Amos, a town he wanted to visit, the other leading to an area in which he had no interest.

Fortunately, an inhabitant was passing by and the stranger started to question him, but then he realized that the man might be of Class A or Class B so the answer would be meaningless.

Assuming that the stranger can ask the inhabitant only one question, what should he ask to locate Amos?

40 minutes

poser group three score

21 _____	26 _____
22 _____	27 _____
23 _____	28 _____
24 _____	29 _____
25 _____	30 _____

total score _____

Poser I. Q.
About 50 is average
*   65-75 is exceptional*
Over 75 is outstanding

poser group four

score 10, 7, 3 or 0
score card on page 32

32.

Two trains are 750 miles apart. One train is traveling at 110 miles an hour and the other at 90 miles an hour.

If the trains are traveling directly toward each other, how far apart will they be exactly one hour before they meet?

3 minutes

33.

There are two "heavy" coins of equal weight and two "lighter" coins of equal weight, all of which are indistinguishable in appearance.

How can the heavy and light coins be positively identified in two weighings on a balance scale?

5 minutes

34.

As a prize, a contest winner is to draw out 1 bill at a time from a box containing 10 five-dollar bills, 10 ten-dollar bills, and 10 twenty-dollar bills. The drawing ends when 3 bills of the same denomination are drawn and, of course, the contest winner keeps whatever he has drawn.

What is the largest sum of money that can be won under these conditions?

4 minutes

35.

How can a novice chess player engage two experts in simultaneous play and be assured of losing not more than one of the two games?

5 minutes

36.

A right-hand glove is turned inside out and then put on the left hand. Where will the fabric of the glove which normally touches the palm of the right hand be found?

Will it be touching the palm, touching the back of the hand, on the palm side facing out, or on the back of the hand side facing out? (Naturally, you are not permitted to use an actual glove.)

15 minutes

37.

A man about to be executed was given an opportunity to make a last statement. If he made a true statement, he would be hung; if a false one, he would be beheaded.

What statement did the doomed man make which prevented the executioner from performing his duty?

10 minutes

38.

A man wished to divide $1,500.00 among his grand-children. Instead of dividing the money equally, he was obliged, because of a long-standing superstition about the number 3, to make a most peculiar distribution among the children.

He would only divide the money if each child could get an amount made up by multiplying 3's. A child could get $3.00, $3 \times 3 = \$9.00$, $3 \times 3 \times 3 = \$27.00$, etc., but no other amounts. And even among the allowable amounts, each could be given to no more than two children.

How much money did each of the children get?

15 minutes

39.

You owe me $1.50. In settlement, I agree to buy from you, for $1.75, a book of posers which is actually worth more. I, therefore give you 25¢ and we consider the matter closed.

At this point, I discover that the book did not belong to you at all but to someone else. In order to keep the book, I must pay the real owner the true value of the book which is $2.95.

Assuming that I cannot get any reimbursement from you, how much did I lose?

15 minutes

40.

A group of children at camp were to be taken down to the lake for swimming practice and in order to keep the trip orderly, they were instructed to line up so that each had a partner. This arrangement, however, was unsatisfactory because one child was left without a partner. Rearranging them in rows of 3, then 5, and then in rows of 7, proved equally unsatisfactory because in each case one additional child would have been required to get a complete formation.

How many children were in the group? (We will assume that a group larger than 300 would have been referred to as a mob.)

20 minutes

poser group four score

31 _____	36 _____
32 _____	37 _____
33 _____	38 _____
34 _____	39 _____
35 _____	40 _____

total score _____

Poser I. Q.
About 50 is average
  65-75 is exceptional
 Over 75 is outstanding

poser group five

score 10, 7, 3 or 0
score card on page 40

41.

A man bought 6 apples and 5 pears. He ate all but 4 apples and 2 pears.

Did he have more apples or pears left?

2 minutes

42.

As a reward, a father promised his son 5 cents for each arithmetic problem he did correctly, but for every one the boy did incorrectly he would have to pay 8 cents back to his father.

In total, the son worked on 26 problems (not counting the problem of figuring out who owed whom money at the end) and, as it turned out, neither owed the other anything.

How many problems did the boy solve correctly?

4 minutes

43.

tailors

If 5 girls can sew 5 dresses in 5 days, how many girls *tailors* would it take to sew 50 dresses in 50 days?

5 minutes

44.

A fruit dealer had a stock of watermelons which he sold
to three customers. The first bought ½ his stock plus ½
of a watermelon. The second bought ½ the remaining
stock plus ½ of a watermelon. After a similar, final sale,
the dealer had no fruit left nor had it been necessary for
him to cut any watermelons in half.

How many melons did he have originally?

10 minutes

45.

Five pennies are placed in a circle on a table so that each
penny touches the pennies on either side of it. The coins
are to be removed by two players who take turns. Each
player is allowed to take 1 penny or 2 if they touch each
other. Two pennies which do not touch cannot be removed
in 1 move. The object of the game is to be the player who
takes the last penny.

If both players make the best possible moves available
to them, should the player who moves first or the player
who moves second win?

8 minutes

46.

Let us assume that a team consists of 3 people: 1 man, 1 woman, and 1 child.

How many different teams, of this composition, can be made from 3 men, 3 women, and 3 children?

10 minutes

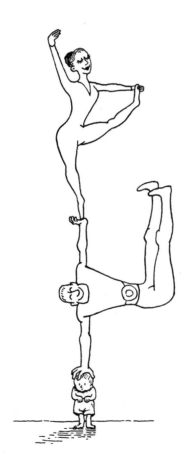

47.

Poker players sometimes have each player "ante," that is, put a certain amount of money into the pot before the deal begins. This practice discourages conservative players from dropping out before they have invested any money. As an alternative, the dealer only can ante, provided each player deals the same number of times.

Under the dealer ante system, 5 players start a game. The first and second deals have been completed, each dealer having put up $5.00, when a new player arrives and seats himself between the first and second dealers. The game is to continue with each of the 3 remaining, original players dealing in turn to complete the first round. However, the new player doesn't want to wait for 3 additional deals but prefers to start playing immediately.

What changes should be made in the ante arrangement which will be fair to both the new and original players? (There is more than one solution.)

15 minutes

48.

A ball is dropped from a height of 200 feet. It hits the ground and rebounds, hits the ground and rebounds, etc.

If the rebound is always 1/10 of the height from which it fell, what is the total distance, to the nearest foot, through which the ball traveled before it came to rest?

15 minutes

49.

Three men left their hats on a rack when they arrived for a party. On the way home, the men were not, for some reason, in condition to tell one hat from another.

If the men each took a hat at random, what is the chance that each got his own hat, 1 in 2, 1 in 4, 1 in 6, 1 in 8, or 1 in 10?

15 minutes

50.

Two faulty clocks both read twelve o'clock. One clock gains a minute each hour while the other loses a minute every hour.

In how many hours will both clocks again show the identical time?

20 minutes

poser group five score

41 _____		46 _____	
42 _____		47 _____	
43 _____		48 _____	
44 _____		49 _____	
45 _____		50 _____	

total score _____

Poser I. Q.
About 50 is average
 65-75 is exceptional
 Over 75 is outstanding

poser group six

score 10, 7, 3 or 0
score card on page 48

51.

A owes $3.00 to B; B owes $2.00 to C; and C owes $1.00 to D.

If A absconds and the others, therefore, refuse to pay their debts, how much do B, C, and D each gain or lose?

3 minutes

52.

At a certain party, every man shook hands twice with each of the other men present and every woman shook hands twice with each of the other women present.

If every man shook hands 8 times and every woman 10 times, how many people attended the party?

3 minutes

53.

At Christmas time, the parents of a large family distributed a stock of toys to their children. Each child got 3 except one child who got only 2. If each child had gotten only 2, 10 toys would have been left over.

How many toys were in the group?

4 minutes

54.

Working alone, a man ~~can~~ *carpenter* complete a job in 3 days, but it takes another ~~man~~ *carpenter* 6 days to do the same work.

How long will it take both ~~men~~ *carpenters*, working together, to complete the job if they each continue to work at their customary rates?

10 minutes

55.

There are 6 coins, 3 "heavy" ones and 3 "light" ones which all look alike and cannot be distinguished by appearance from each other. The 3 heavy coins are all of the same weight while the 3 light ones are also identical in weight.

How can 2 of the 3 heavy coins be positively identified in 2 weighings on a balance scale?

10 minutes

56.

In a certain office building with 7 floors, there is an elevator which operates in a rather peculiar way. It cannot reverse its direction until it gets to the 7th floor or to the 1st floor. Thus, if the elevator completed a move from the 1st floor to the 3rd floor, it would respond to a call on the 2nd floor by going up to the 7th, then down to the 2nd. On the other hand, if it had come to the 3rd from above, then it would have descended directly to the 2nd.

Two friends had offices in this building, one on the 6th floor and the other on the 3rd. One day they both rang for the elevator at exactly the same instant.

Assuming the position and direction of the elevator at that time to be purely a matter of chance, which man had the best chance of getting the elevator first?

15 minutes

57.

There are 3 piles of markers, one containing 5, the second containing 4, and the third 2 markers. A game is played in which each of two players removes, in turn, as many markers from any 1 pile as he wishes including the elimination of a whole pile. The object of the game is to remove the last marker.

What is the only correct move for the player who is about to move to assure that he will win, no matter what the other player does?

15 minutes

58.

Suppose that all X's are also Y's, but only some Y's are Z's.

Which one of the following statements is true?
1. No X's can be Z's.
2. If something is not a Y, it is also not an X.
3. If something is a Z, it cannot be an X.

15 minutes

59.

In a box, a gambler has four $10.00 bills and one $20.00 bill. For the payment of an amount which will yield the gambler a substantial profit, he will let you put your hand into the box and, without looking, take out and keep one of the bills.

If the gambler was an honest man and the game was fair, how much should be paid for this opportunity?

15 minutes

60.

Seven coins are placed on a table. Each of 2 players takes from 1 to 3 coins away when his turn comes, the object of the game being to have an odd number of coins when all have been taken.

What move should the first man make to assure that he will win?

20 minutes

poser group six score

51 _____		56 _____
52 _____		57 _____
53 _____		58 _____
54 _____		59 _____
55 _____		60 _____

total score _____

Poser I. Q.
About 50 is average
*   65-75 is exceptional*
Over 75 is outstanding

poser group seven

score 10, 7, 3 or 0
score card on page 58

61.

In the drawing below, capital H's represent houses in which there are no children. The houses represented by small h's do have children living in them. S represents a swimming pool which is shared by the people who live in all 8 houses.

In order to protect the children, it is desired to build a continuous fence so that the people in the H houses will be inside the fence and the people in the h houses will have to go through a gate in the fence to get to the pool.

How should this fence be built?

5 minutes

62.

Coins are placed in the frames, "heads" and "tails" showing, as in the diagram below. Coins can be moved to empty frames which are directly above, below, to the side, or diagonally adjacent.

What is the smallest number of moves needed to interchange the "heads" and "tails"?

3 minutes

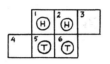

63.

A college dormitory was designed as shown in the diagram below. Each room was supposed to accommodate 3 students for a total of 24 in the eight-room group. The charge-of-quarters was in the habit of making a night check by simply counting the number of students on each side of the square, and if the total was 9 on each side, it was assumed that all the students were accounted for.

It soon became apparent to the students that if 4 of them were not present, they could still arrange themselves so that the count of 9 on each side would still be obtained.

What arrangement, using only 20 students, will give the necessary count of 9 on each side of the dormitory?

5 minutes

3	3	3
3		3
3	3	3

64.

Shown below is a position in a new variety of tit-tat-toe. Each player moves in the normal way, but the object of the game is to get 5 X's or O's in a row, either across, down, or on the diagonal. Play has progressed to the point shown in the diagram, each player having moved 10 times. It is now X's move.

How should he move so that he must win in exactly 3 moves assuming O makes the best moves available to him.

5 minutes

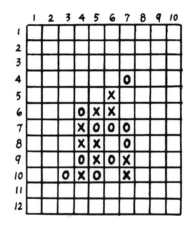

65.

The object of this game is to create a "chain" of 3 B's or W's. Black's chain must connect the 2 sides marked "black" and white must try to connect the 2 sides marked "white." As usual, each player moves in turn.

Play has progressed as shown below and it is now white's move.

What should white's next move be to assure that he will win no matter how B responds?

15 minutes

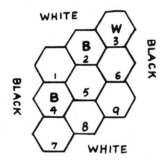

66.

In the arrangement shown in the diagram, 9 coins have been placed so that they form 8 rows of 3.

Can you rearrange these 9 coins to form 10 rows of 3?

12 minutes

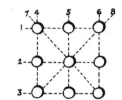

67.

*Shown below is an area made up of 3 identical squares.
How can the artist draw some additional lines so that 4
areas of identical shape and size are created?*

20 minutes

68.

On the board below, markers can be placed not in the boxes but on the intersections. Each of 2 players places markers, in turn, until 3 have been placed by each player, then the first player must move 1 of the markers already placed to an adjacent intersection. (You cannot move a marker along a diagonal.) The second player then moves 1 of his markers to a vacant, adjacent intersection, etc. The object of the game is to get 3 markers in a row, either across, down or on a diagonal.

If A moves first at location 5, should A always win or can B force a draw assuming both players make the best possible moves?

25 minutes

69.

A long-division example was worked out on a piece of paper which, unfortunately, got wet and the only legible number remaining was the 8 as shown below. The numbers which could not be read are shown by X's.

Can you supply the missing numbers?

25 minutes

```
            X X 8 X X
      X X ) X X X X X X X
            X X X
              X X
              X X
                X X X
                X X X
```

70.

Can you place 6 markers in the 6 by 6 grid shown below so that no 2 markers are on the same horizontal, vertical, or diagonal line?

25 minutes

poser group seven score

61 _____   66 _____

62 _____   67 _____

63 _____   68 _____

64 _____   69 _____

65 _____   70 _____

total score _____

Poser I. Q.
About 50 is average
65-75 is exceptional
Over 75 is outstanding

groups one to seven—average score

group 1 _____ (*p. 8*)   5 _____ (*p. 40*)

2 _____ (*p. 16*)   6 _____ (*p. 48*)

3 _____ (*p. 24*)   7 _____ (*p. 57*)

4 _____ (*p. 32*)   total _____

AVERAGE SCORE (total divided by 7) _____

super poser group eight

score 10, 7, 3, or 0
score card on page 66

71.

A restaurant, famous for its rolls, doesn't charge for them if the diner eats a reasonable number. There is a charge, however, for each roll eaten above the magic number.

A husband and wife who loved the crispy rolls, together consumed 13 and were charged 60 cents. Had one person eaten them, the charge would have been $1.60.

How many rolls can a person eat without being charged?

15 minutes

72.

When a census taker found no one at home in a certain house, he asked a neighbor to tell him how many people lived there and what their ages were. The neighbor replied that, in addition to a husband and wife whose ages he did not know, there were 4 people living in the house. Their ages, to the nearest year, when multiplied together, total 225. When their ages are added together, they total the number painted on the front door of the house.

The census taker, being a good mathematician, tried to work out the 4 ages but soon returned to the neighbor and said, "You haven't given me enough information."

"You're right," replied the neighbor, "I forgot to tell you that John, the oldest, is old enough to vote."

With this additional information, the census taker was able to determine the 4 ages. What were they?

20 minutes

73.

Two swimmers start at the same time at each end of a pool and swim toward the opposite ends. When they pass each other, they are 40 yards from the east end. The swimmers continue to the ends of the pool, turn around and swim in the opposite directions. This time they meet 20 yards from the west end.

How long is the pool?

25 minutes

74.

During the course of a vacation, there were 11 days in which there was some rain. If it rained in the morning, however, the afternoon was always clear and if it rained in the afternoon, those mornings had always been clear. In total, there were 9 clear mornings and 12 clear afternoons. How many days were entirely without rain?

15 minutes

75.

An ancient potentate frequently condemned to death those whom he no longer favored. However, he amused himself by giving his victims a chance to live if they were lucky or smart enough to take advantage of the opportunity he gave them to escape death.

One victim was handed 8 vials filled with hemlock and 8 filled with water. He was told that after he had put the vials into 2 boxes, someone would draw out 1 vial from one of the boxes and he would have to drink its contents.

What arrangement of the vials in the 2 boxes will give the condemned man the best chance of avoiding the hemlock?

15 minutes

76.

An officer on horseback starts at the back of a column of marching men and rides to the front of the column. He then turns around and rides back to the rear of the column.

If the rider travels 3 times as fast as the column moves and the column is 100 yards long, how far has the column moved by the time the officer has completed his tour of inspection?

25 minutes

77.

A well known arithmetic poser deals with a son at college who wired his father:

```
    S E N D
    M O R E
  ─────────
  M O N E Y
```

If each letter in the wire is replaced by the correct number, the wire becomes a correct exercise in addition as follows:

```
      9 5 6 7
      1 0 8 5
  ───────────
  1 0 6 5 2
```

It is not commonly known, however, that the father's reply was also in the form of a wire which resolves itself into an addition example:

```
      U S E
    L E S S
  ─────────
  S O N N Y
```

Can you determine the replacement numbers which will make this a correct sum? (There are 3 correct solutions.)

25 minutes

78.

Two men, A and B, each throw a die.

What is the chance that A will throw a higher number than B, 5 chances out of 8; 5 out of 10; 5 out of 12; or 5 out of 15?

20 minutes

79.

A sister and brother usually come home from school at approximately the same time. The boy always rings the doorbell, but the girl rings the doorbell half the time and the other half of the time uses her key. One afternoon, the doorbell rang and one of the two children was admitted by the mother, but she didn't notice which child it was.

What is the chance that the other child will ring the doorbell, 1 out of 2; 2 out of 3; 3 out of 4; 4 out of 5; or 5 out of 6?

25 minutes

80.

A customer came into a tavern with a 5-pint and a 3-pint jug, and asked the bartender for 1 pint of beer in each jug. The bartender had a barrel which contained 15 pints but no measuring devices whatsoever.

He soon realized that it would take considerable ingenuity to work out the method for performing this feat, but, being a confirmed poser addict, he finally came up with the answer. It must be noted that he found it expedient to consume 13 pints of beer in the course of solving the poser because the only other alternative (perish the thought) was to waste the beer.

How did the bartender get 1 pint into each jug?

1 hour

super poser group eight score

71 _____	76 _____
72 _____	77 _____
73 _____	78 _____
74 _____	79 _____
75 _____	80 _____

total score _____

Super Poser I. Q.
About 50 is startling
65-75 is amazing
Over 75 is fantastic

solutions

1.

The cost would be $250 because each line costs $50 and it requires 5 lines to create 6 lanes.

2.

The water in the "middle" full glass is emptied into the "middle" empty glass, making the new arrangement "empty, full, empty, full, empty, full."

3.

A one-way street cannot end in a dead end. If it did, cars entering the street could not legally get out.

4.

This cannot be done if all the cigarettes lie on 1 surface. In 3 dimensions, the solution is as shown in the diagram below.

5.

The gambler is behind. Even if he had made only 2 bets, won 1 and lost 1, he would have been behind. For example, starting with $10, if he wins then loses, he will have had $15 after winning and $7.50 after losing. Had he lost first, then won, he would have had $5 after losing, and the same $7.50 after winning. As a matter of fact, it makes no difference in what order the "wins" and "loses" occur; he will be behind the same amount under any circumstances.

6.

The "inside" man washed 8 more windows than the "outside" man. It makes no difference how many windows there were, but let's assume there were 20 insides and 20 outsides. Then the inside man must have washed 16 insides and 8 outsides for a total of 24 and the other man washed the remaining 16.

7.

The writing will be on the front of the duplicate but not as written. If held upside-down in front of a mirror, the original image will appear.

8.

It would be necessary to select 5 shoes. If 4 "lefts" were selected, there would have to be at least 1 of each color among them. Any "right" would then have to create a pair.

9.

The glass should be tilted so that the liquid just touches the lip of the glass. By noting whether the surface of the liquid at the other end cuts the side of the glass, bottom of the glass or just in between, it can be determined whether there is more than half, less than half or just half of a full glass remaining.

10.

The first man marks off an area which he considers to be ⅓ of the total. The second man, if he feels the marked area is more than ⅓ of the total, reduces the size of the marked-off area to what he considers to be ⅓ of the total. The third man can then take this reduced area as his share or let the second man keep it. In either case, the remaining two men divide the remainder of the land in accordance with King Solomon's principle. If the second man considers the original division to be just or less than ⅓, he "passes" and the third man has the option of taking the marked-off area or leaving it to the first man who then must take it as his share. Again, the remaining two men follow Solomon's procedure.

If the land were to be divided into more than 3 parts, the same procedure would be used except that each man in turn would be given the opportunity to "pass" or reduce the area being considered at that time. Each time an area is assigned, the procedure starts again until every man has his equitable portion.

11.

The two boys row across and one boy rows back. Now, one man rows across and the boy who was left on the other side rows back. Both boys row across and one boy rows back. The second man now rows across, etc.

12.

They will both show the correct time at six o'clock. when the accurate clock is at 1:00, the other is at 11:00; at 2:00, the faulty clock is at 10:00, etc., until at 6:00, the two clocks will agree.

13.

The slower burning candle will be twice as long as the faster burning one after two hours. At that time, the slower burning one will still have ⅔ of its length left while the other will have only ⅓ left.

14.

From the third and fourth statements, the King is spotted between a Heart and a Spade. The second statement identifies the King as a Diamond and the first statement makes the Jack a Heart and the Queen a Spade.

15.

One 2″ outlet will empty the bathtub faster, as illustrated in the diagram below. Note that a cross section of the 2″ outlet has more area (twice as much, to be exact) than the combined areas of the 1″ outlets.

16.

He would have said, "It's a portrait of my daughter."

17.

The right lane is the best (in countries with left-hand drive), but the answer "left or right lane" is acceptable. If the left lane disappears, the traffic in the left and middle lanes will be slowed down. If the right lane disappears, the traffic in the right and middle lanes will be affected. In both cases, the middle-lane traffic will be slowed. Therefore, traveling in the left or right lane gives a 50% chance of being unaffected by the squeeze and a 50% chance of being no worse off than being in the middle lane. Where the driver sits on the left, it is easier and usually faster to squeeze left than right, so the right-hand lane is preferable to the left.

18.

The rifle can be placed, on the diagonal, in a box each of whose dimensions is one yard.

19.

The ship that started from New York is sailing twice as fast as the other. When the two ships met, the New York ship had come twice as far as the liverpool ship and, therefore, it will take the Liverpool ship, which travels only half as fast as the New York ship, four times as long to complete the crossing.

20.

Three men would be sufficient. After 1 day's journey, one man gives a day's supplies to each of the other two men and with the supplies remaining he returns to the starting point. The two other men now have full packs again and go on for another day. At that time, one man gives a day's supplies to the other. The latter now has 4 days' supplies with which he can complete the crossing, and the other man has a 2 days' supply, sufficient to get back to the starting point.

21.

Twelve socks must be taken. The first 10 selected might all be black, but then the next 2 must be brown.

22.

He made the trip in 3 different taxis, thus avoiding 2 extra charges for crossing boundaries.

23.

The amount of profit or loss cannot be determined. When the bookcase was sold for $40.00 we would have to know how much the merchant had paid for it to know how much he made or lost on the sale. On the repurchase and resale the merchant made a profit of $5.00, but the profit or loss on the whole transaction depends on the original cost of the bookcase which is unknown.

24.

It would take more time. A round trip in still water would take 2 hours, 1 hour going and 1 hour returning. Going into the wind at 15 miles per hour, the one way trip of 30 miles would take 2 hours so the complete trip would have to take longer than that.

25.

At the beginning of the trip, both cars have the same distance to go. By the time the slower car has gone half way, the other car has completed the whole trip. Just before the faster car completes the trip, let's say when it has only one foot to go, the slower car still has more than five miles to go. Therefore, there is a time when the slower car has not only 5,000 times as far, but any desired number of times as far to go as the faster car.

26.

If A's statement is true, then B's must be false and C's must be true, giving two true statements when only one is allowed. Therefore, A's statement must be false making him the person who committed the crime and only B's statement is true.

27.

He started with $7.00. Since the man had no money left after the third purchase, he must have had $4.00 upon entering the third store. This means he must have had $12.00 after borrowing from the second merchant and $6.00 before he made this loan. Going back one more step, he must have had $14.00 after borrowing from the first merchant and $7.00 before borrowing from anybody.

28.
The father ties one end of the rope to the tree stump and, holding the other end, walks around the lake to the other side. In this way, the rope will be stretched across the lake and the son will be able to grab hold of it. The raft can then be pulled ashore by the father or son or both working together.

29.

30.
The question is, "What would a person, not of your Class, answer if I asked him if this road (pointing to one) led to Amos?"
If the road did lead to Amos, the truth teller would answer "No" because a liar would answer "No" when asked if the road led to Amos. A liar would also answer "No" because a truth teller would really answer "Yes" and the liar, therefore, would lie about the truth teller's answer. Similarly, both classes would answer "Yes" if the stranger had pointed to the road which did not lead to Amos.

31.
Forty divided by ¼ is 160 (not 10) which makes the answer 167.

32.
They will be 200 miles apart. Since one train travels at 110 and the other at 90 miles per hour, one hour before they meet they must be 110 plus 90 or 200 miles apart. The fact that the trains were 750 miles apart at the beginning is of no particular importance.

33.

Two coins are weighed against each other. If the scale does not balance, one heavy and one light coin have been identified. Weighing the other two coins against each other will identify the other heavy and light coins. If the scale balances on the first weighing, both coins must be heavy or both light. Weighing one of these against either of the remaining coins will determine whether both are heavy or light.

34.

The best that can happen would be for the contest winner to draw 2 fives, 2 tens and 2 twenties and, on the last draw, another twenty for a total of $90.00.

35.

Against one expert, he plays the white pieces and against the other, he plays the black pieces. Whatever move the first expert makes, playing white, to start the first game, the novice makes the same move in the game against the other expert. When the second expert responds, the novice duplicates the move in the first game. He continues to follow this procedure and since both games are identical, he cannot lose both.

36.

The fabric normally touching the right palm will be on the palm side of the left hand, facing out.

37.

The victim said, "I am going to be beheaded." The executioner could not hang the man because his statement would then be false and he should have been beheaded. Nor could the victim be beheaded for then his statement would be true and he should have been hung.

38.
The possible sums which the grandfather could have given were
$3.00, $9.00, $27.00, $81.00, $243.00 and $729.00. Starting with
the largest sum, two children can get that amount ($729.00) which
uses up $1,458.00. No one can get $243.00 or $81.00 but one child
can get $27.00 which leaves $15.00 for three children. One child
gets $9.00 and two get $3.00 each.

39.
I lost $1.75 consisting of the $1.50 which you owed me originally
plus the additional 25¢ I gave you. The transaction involving the
real owner did not produce any loss since I got $2.95 in value for
the $2.95 I paid.

40.
Complete formations in rows of 2, 3, 5 or 7 could have been made
if there had been one more child. Therefore, 210 children, which is
obtained by multiplying 2 x 3 x 5 x 7, is ~~larger~~ smaller by 1 than the
number of children in the group. There were ~~209~~ children.
211

41.
He had more apples (4) than pears (2) left.

42.
The boy solved 16 problems correctly which netted him 80¢. The 10
he missed cost him the same amount.

43. tailors
If 5 ~~girls~~ tailors can sew 5 dresses in 5 days, 1 ~~girl~~ tailor can sew 1 dress in 5
days, 1 ~~girl~~ tailor can sew 10 dresses in 50 days and, therefore, 5 ~~girls~~ tailors
can sew 50 dresses in 50 days.

44.
Since the third sale exhausted his stock, he must have had just 1
watermelon left when the third customer bought ½ of 1, plus ½,

75

which is 1. Before the second sale, he must have had 3 ($\frac{1}{2}$ of 3, plus $\frac{1}{2}$ = 2, leaving 1). Before the second sale, he must have had 7 ($\frac{1}{2}$ of 7, plus $\frac{1}{2}$ = 4, leaving 3). The answer is 7.

45.

The player who moves second should win. If the first player, A, takes 1 penny, the correct response by B is to take the 2 opposite pennies, leaving 2 separated pennies, only 1 of which A can take on his next move and, therefore, B gets the last one. If, on the other hand, A takes 2 pennies on his first move, then B should take the 1 opposite penny leaving the situation exactly as before and again B wins.

46.

If a team consisted of only a woman and a child, then 9 teams could be made up from just the 3 women and the 3 children by matching each woman with each of the 3 children in turn. Now, adding each of the 3 men, in turn, to the 9 teams gives 9 times 3 or 27 teams consisting of a man, a woman and a child.

47.

The simplest solution is to have the 3 remaining, original players ante $5.00 while the new player puts up $1.00 for each of 3 deals. After the first round is completed, the ante can, as before, be left at $5.00 or changed to some other amount, perhaps $6.00 if the intent is to have the equivalent of a $1.00 ante per person.
Another solution can be obtained by reasoning that since 2 players have each already put up $5.00 and 3 others have put up nothing, $2.00 should be given up by each of the latter so that the first 2 dealers can get back $3.00 each and each player will thus have invested $2.00. After this distribution, it can be assumed that a new game is starting, and each player must then deal the same number of times.

48.

After the initial drop of 200 feet, the ball rebounds and then falls 1/10 the previous height, so that the additional distances through which the ball travels would be:

2 times 20
2 times 2
2 times   .2
2 times   .02, etc.

or a total of 2 times 22.22 etc., which is 44 feet to the nearest foot and so the total distance is 244 feet to the nearest foot.

49.

The first man to pick up a hat has 1 out of 3 chances of getting his own. If he is successful, the second man has 1 out of 2 chances of getting his own hat. The third man then will necessarily get his own hat. Therefore, there is 1 chance out of 6 for each to get his own hat.

50.

Each hour the clocks get 2 minutes farther apart. After 30 hours, they will be 1 hour apart. Now, since 12 hours apart is the same as being together again, 30 times 12 or 360 hours will be required to bring them together again.

51.

By absconding, A gained $3.00 which is the total lost by B, C and D, each having lost $1.00.

52.

Since each man shook hands 8 times, there must have been 5 men present; each woman shook hands 10 times so there were 6 women present for a total of 11.

53.

By taking 1 toy away from each child who originally had 3, 10 toys were collected so that there must have been 10 children who had 3 toys each. The total number of toys was 3 times 10 plus 2 or 32.

54.

The first man can complete $\frac{1}{3}$ of the job in 1 day; the second man can complete $\frac{1}{6}$ of the job in 1 day. Together, they can complete $\frac{1}{3}$ plus $\frac{1}{6}$ or $\frac{1}{2}$ the job in 1 day. Consequently, they can complete the job together in 2 days.

55.

Three coins are weighed against the remaining 3 coins. The side of the scale which contains 3 heavy coins or 2 heavy ones must, of course, go down. From these 3 coins, any 2 are selected and weighed against each other. If the scale balances, both coins must be heavy. If the scale does not balance, 1 coin is heavy and the other heavy coin is the third of the 3 coins chosen on the first weighing which is off the scale on the second weighing.

56.

The man on the 3rd floor had the better chance of getting the elevator first. If the elevator was headed up between the 1st and 3rd floors or down between the 6th and 1st floors, the man on the 3rd floor would catch it first. The 6th floor occupant would be successful in getting it first if the elevator was headed up between the 3rd and 7th floors or down between the 7th and 6th. The chances are 7 against 5 in favor of the 3rd floor man.

57.

The only winning move is to remove 1 marker from the pile of 2 leaving 1. To prove that this is the winning move, it will be helpful to examine first the situation when there are 3 piles consisting of 1, 2 and 3 markers. This position is losing for the person who must move because whatever move is made, the other player can reduce the piles to 2 having the same number of markers which is obviously losing for the person who must then move.

Keeping in mind that 1, 2, 3 is losing for the player who must move, we can now examine the position 1, 4, 5. Whatever move is made from this position, the other player can either reduce the piles to 1, 2, 3 or to 2 piles containing the same number of markers, either of which, as we know, is losing for the player who must move.

It can also be readily seen that any original move other than removing 1 from the 2 pile will give the advantage to the second player who will be able to move into the 1, 2, 3 or 2 identical pile arrangements.

58.
Only the second statement is true. This can easily be seen if we substitute something meaningful for X, Y and Z. For example, the original statement could be: All numbers from 1 to 10 (X's) are also numbers from 1 to 100 (Y's), but only some numbers from 1 to 100 (Y's) are odd numbers (Z's).

Statement 1 then becomes: No numbers from 1 to 10 can be odd.

Statement 2 becomes: If a number is not between 1 and 100, it is not between 1 and 10.

Statement 3 becomes: If a number is odd, it can't be between 1 and 10.

Obviously, only statement 2 is true.

59.
Since it is equally likely that any of the bills will be taken out, the $20.00 bill will be taken out, on the average, 1 time in every 5 draws. Or, to put it differently, one can expect to take out $60.00 in 5 draws. Therefore, a fair price to pay is $12.00 which will total $60.00 for 5 draws.

60.
He should take 2 coins, leaving 5. If his opponent takes 1, the response is to take 3 and end up with 5. If the opponent takes 2, the first man takes the remaining 3 and again ends up with 5.

Finally, if the opponent takes 3, the first man takes 1 and ends up with 3. If the first man's initial move is 1 or 3, the response of 2 and 3 respectively will win for the second man.

61.

62.
Only 5 moves are required. Move the coin in box number 2 to box number 3; 5 to 2; 1 to 5; 6 to 1; 3 to 6.

63.

Four students occupy each of the 4 corner rooms while only 1 student remains in each of the other 4 rooms.

64.

X moves at row 8, column 3 forcing O to move to row 9, column 2. Now X moves at row 8, column 2 forming 4 X's in a row with open spaces at both ends. Since O can protect only 1 end, X wins on his third move.

65.
The correct move for white is in box #5. After this move white is threatening to go into #6 after which #8 or #9 completes the chain. Black can force white's next move, but always into winning positions. If black moves into #1 white is forced into #6, but this is where he intended to go anyway and he wins. If black goes into #8 white is forced into #9, but then he must win because both #1 and #6 will complete the chain. If black goes into #9 #8 is forced on A, but again either #1 or #6 completes the

chain. If black goes into #6 white goes into #1 and wins by #8 or #9. Black in #7 is meaningless and white wins in any number of ways. It should be noted that any move by white other than into #5 leads to an easy victory for black.

66.

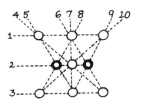

67.
Since the area must be divided into 4 identical parts, each part will be equal to ¾ of one of the squares. This line of reasoning suggests the solution shown below.

68.
A should always win. If A places his first marker at 5, B can either place his marker in a corner (1, 3, 7 or 9) or in the middle of a side (2, 4, 6 or 8). If B moves to a corner, let's say to 1, A's response is to place a marker at 6 forcing B to move to 4. A then places a marker at 7, forcing B to commit his third marker at 3. A's next 2 moves, no matter what B does, are to move from 5 to 8 and from 6 to 9. If B moves to the middle of a side, let's say to 2, A places a marker at 7, forcing B to respond at 3. A then places a marker at 1 and B must commit his third marker at 4. A will now win by moving the marker at 7 to 8 and then to 9.

69.
The numbers in the 2nd and 4th digits of the quotient must be 0's since an additional digit of the dividend had to be brought

down. Also since 8 times the 2 digit divisor gives a 2 digit product, the 1st and last digits of the quotient must be 9's since they give 3 digit products when multiplied by the 2 digit divisor. The whole quotient must therefore be 90809. The divisor must be 12 because only that number will give a 2 digit product when multiplied by 8 and a 3 digit number when multiplied by 9. Multiplying 90809 by 12 will give the dividend and the other illegible numbers can then be obtained by performing the division.

The complete solution is:

$$
\begin{array}{r}
90809 \\
12\overline{)1089708} \\
108 \\
\hline
97 \\
96 \\
\hline
108 \\
108 \\
\hline
\end{array}
$$

70.

71.

Since an extra $1.00 would have been charged had there been only one diner, this must be the cost of eating a "quota" of rolls. Had there been a charge for all the rolls consumed, another $1.00 would have been added to the check making a total of $2.60 for 13 rolls, so each roll must cost 20¢ and the 60¢ was the charge for 3 rolls. The "quota" must be 5 rolls per person.

72.

There are only 9 ways in which 4 ages can be multiplied together to give 225 as follows:

```
225 x  1 x 1 x 1  sum  is  228
 75 x  3 x 1 x 1   "    "   80
 45 x  5 x 1 x 1   "    "   52
 25 x  3 x 3 x 1   "    "   32*
 25 x  9 x 1 x 1   "    "   36
 15 x  5 x 3 x 1   "    "   24
 15 x 15 x 1 x 1   "    "   32*
  9 x  5 x 5 x 1   "    "   20
  5 x  5 x 3 x 3   "    "   16
```

The census taker had only to write down the 9 possibilities and then find the one in which the ages totaled to the house number. Evidently, the reason he had trouble was that the house number was 32 which left the issue still in doubt. The additional information resolved the problem. The ages were 25, 3, 3 and 1.

73.
From the diagram below it can be seen that when the swimmers met for the first time they had jointly covered 1 length of the pool, but when they met for the second time they had jointly covered the length of the pool 3 times. The swimmer who had swum 40 yards at the first meeting must have swum 120 yards at the second meeting. The distance he covered was 20 yards more than 1 length of the pool, so the pool must be 100 yards long.

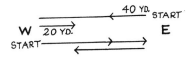

74.
Since there were 9 clear mornings and 12 clear afternoons, the 11 days on which there was some rain must divide into 7 mornings and 4 afternoons, making the length of the vacation 16 days. There having been some rain on 11 days, 5 days must have been entirely without rain.

75.

He should put 1 vial of water in one box and all the others in the other box. In this way he has a "50–50" chance of having the box with the water only chosen and go free, and even if the other box is selected his chances are still almost "50–50."

76.

When the officer is moving in the same direction as the column he arrives at the head of the column when he has traveled 150 yards because the column will have advanced 50 yards. When he travels in the opposite direction he reaches the rear after riding 75 yards since the column moved forward 25 yards. The column will have moved 75 yards by the time the officer completes his inspection tour.

77.

It is apparent at once that S must be 1, L is 9 and O is 0. Also, since 2 S's add to N, N must be 2. Now substituting the known numbers, the sum becomes:

$$
\begin{array}{r}
U\ 1\ E \\
9\ E\ 1\ 1 \\
\hline
1\ 0\ 2\ 2\ Y
\end{array}
$$

The values of the remaining letters can be found by trying all possible numbers for any 1 of the remaining letters and following the consequences. For example, E cannot be 1 or 2 because those numbers are already "spoken for." It cannot be 3 because then U would have to be a 9 which also has been "spoken for." Similarly, it will be found that E can be only a 4, 5 or 7 and the 3 resulting solutions are:

$$
\begin{array}{ccc}
814 & 715 & 517 \\
9411 & 9511 & 9711 \\
\hline
10225 & 10226 & 10228
\end{array}
$$

78.

The answer is not 5 out of 10 because there is 1 chance in 6 that they will throw the same number and only 5 chances out of 6 that they will throw different numbers. Of course, there is an equal chance that A's number will be higher than B's or B's higher than A's. Therefore, the chance that A's number will be higher than B's is ½ of 5 out of 6 or 5 chances out of 12.

79.

If we call the brother B and the sister S, ringing the doorbell R, and not ringing the doorbell N, then ordinarily there are 4 equally likely possibilities when the children come home:

BR followed by SR
BR   ″   ″ SN
SR   ″   ″ BR
SN   ″   ″ BR

The last possibility, SN followed by BR, which implies that the sister came home first but did not ring, is impossible in the case we are examining because the bell did ring. This leaves 3 other possibilities in which 2 out of 3 result in the bell being rung again which makes the answer 2 out of 3 that the other child will ring.

80.

First he filled the 5-pint and 3-pint jugs and next he drank the 7 pints left in the barrel. He then poured the contents of the 3-pint jug into the barrel and refilled the 3-pint jug from the 5-pint one. Next he poured the 3 pints from the 3-pint jug into the barrel and transferred the 2 pints remaining in the 5-pint jug into the 3-pint jug. This leaves the 5-pint jug empty, 2 pints in the 3-pint jug and 6 pints in the barrel.
The five-pint jug is now filled from the barrel, leaving 1 pint in the barrel. The 3-pint jug is filled from the 5-pint jug, leaving 4 pints in the 5-pint jug and 3 pints in the 3-pint jug. The latter is consumed by the bartender. Again the 3-pint jug is filled and drunk, leaving 1 pint in the 5-pint jug. Finally, the 1 pint in the barrel is transferred to the 3-pint jug.